To Chris,

Sit back, relax, and enjoy
a very special 60th Birthday.

UP THE
GARDEN PATH

By Norman Thelwell

Three Sheets in the Wind
Up the Garden Path
Compleat Tangler
Play it as it Lies

thelwell.

UP THE
GARDEN PATH

Allison & Busby Limited
12 Fitzroy Mews
London W1T 6DW
www.allisonandbusby.com

First published in 1967.
This edition published in Great Britain by Allison & Busby in 2014.

A CIP catalogue record for this book is available from
the British Library.

10 9 8 7 6 5 4 3 2 1

ISBN 978-0-7490-1706-4

Typeset in 10/15 pt Adobe Caslon Pro by
Allison & Busby Ltd.

The paper used for this Allison & Busby publication
has been produced from trees that have been legally sourced
from well-managed and credibly certified forests.

Printed and bound by
CPI Group (UK) Ltd, Croydon, CR0 4YY

CONTENTS

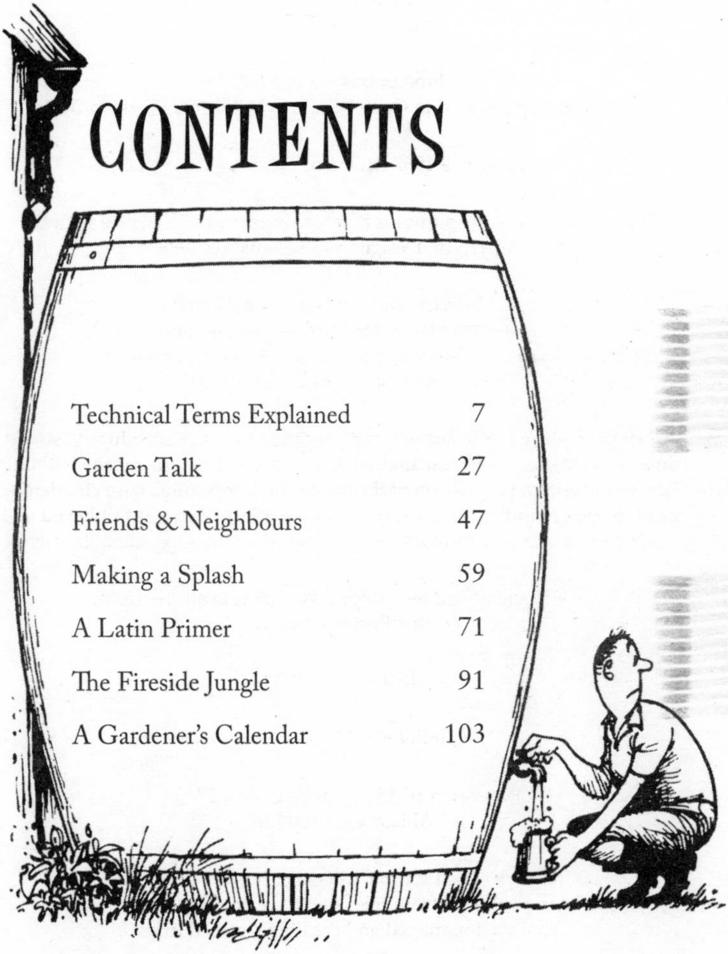

TECHNICAL TERMS
EXPLAINED

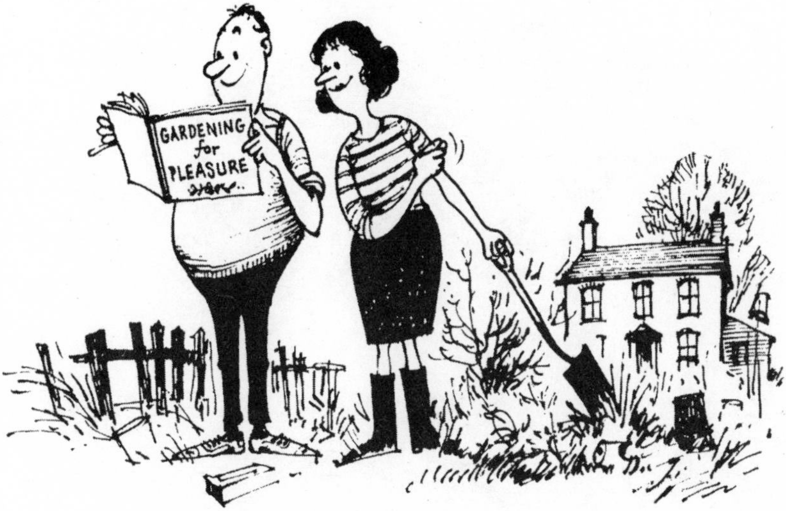
GARDENING
for
PLEASURE

Suckers

Earthing up

Club root

Garden fencing

Mites

Black spot

Freezia

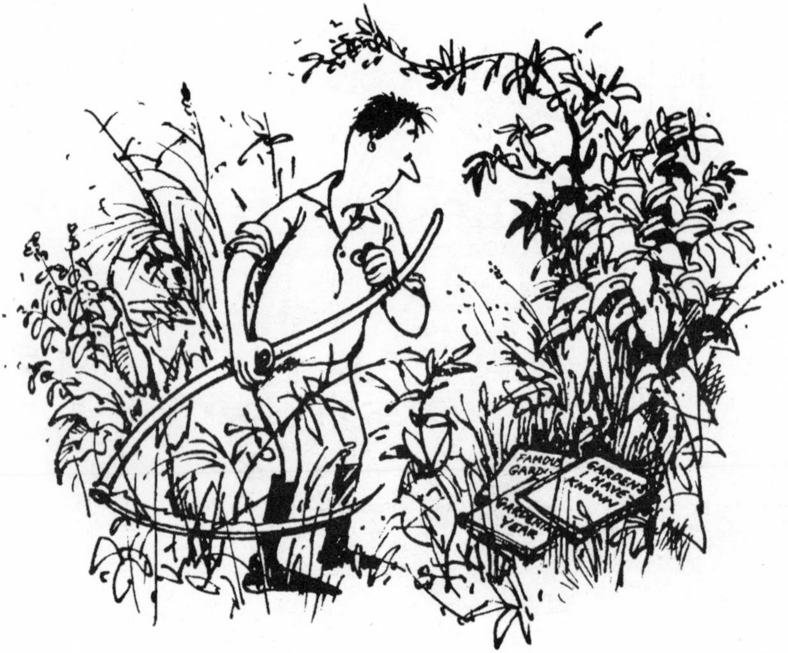
FAMOUS
GARDENS I HAVE KNOWN

Hardy annuals

Hybrid tea

Top dressing

Snow in summer

Phlox

Stone crop

Pesticide

Garden roller

A heavy cropper

Damping off

GARDEN TALK

'I've decided to do some muck spreading.'

'It ran amok.'

'I think I've found your transistor radio.'

'Every damn potato's a freak.'

'Who turned the pressure up?'

'They're creosoting the fence next door.'

'I told you that hanging basket was loose.'

'I'm letting it lie fallow this year.'

'Do you mind if a few reporters come through?'

'. . . And then, beyond the lawns, a lily pool with
fountains and a rose pergola leading to a rustic
summer house . . .'

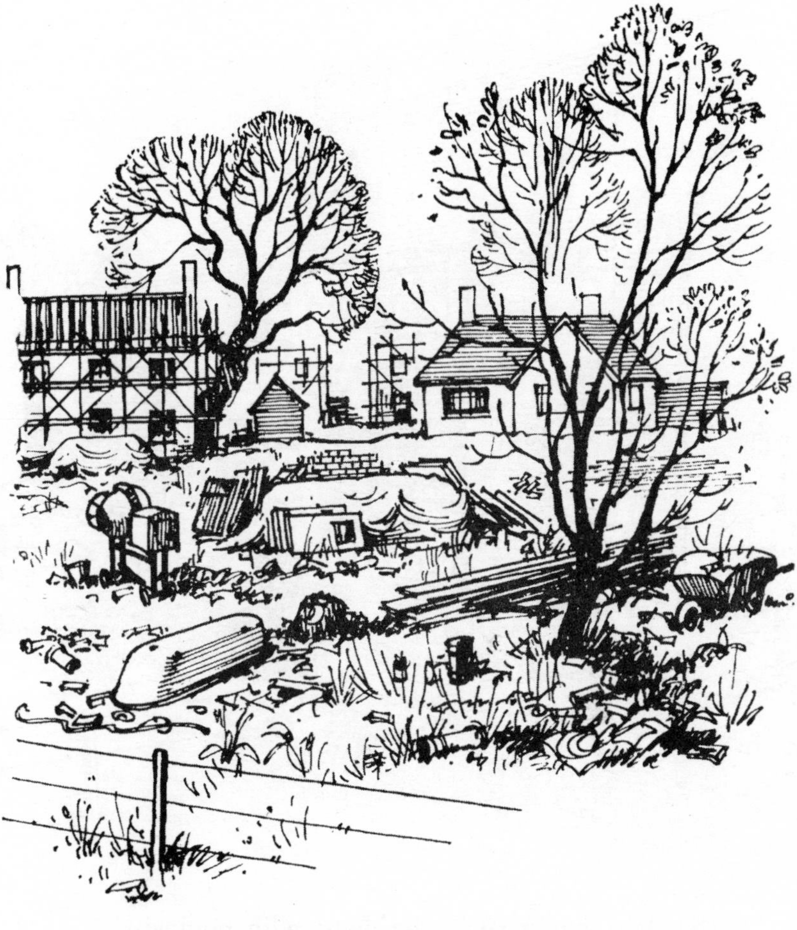

'That was a stupid place to put the lawn mowings.'

'You never liked that concrete gnome, did you?'

'Is that what we pay him seventy pence an hour for?'

'You give up too easily, dear.'

'We climbed three thousand feet up Mont Blanc
to get that one.'

'You've got your foot on my shallots, mate.'

FRIENDS &
NEIGHBOURS

A give-and-take relationship with your neighbour
is essential to the full enjoyment of your garden.

Never criticise his creative efforts . . .

or insist on giving him unsolicited advice.

When he is in trouble, be prepared to help out of course

but you should respect his privacy at all times.

If his animals should stray – let him know by all means

but don't be vindictive.

Avoid constant borrowing.

A householder is entitled to remove any object
that encroaches on his property . . .

but it MUST be returned to the rightful owner.

MAKING A SPLASH

For those who have not tried it before,
water gardening can be great fun.

Some people get pleasure from working out
ambitious schemes . . .

others prefer the modern, easy way.

A fountain is certain to provide endless delight.

An occasional cleanout should prevent
unpleasant smells

but incorrect stocking can upset the balance
of your water.

You will be surprised by the wild birds
that will appear in your garden

. . . and many other things you have not
seen there before.

One thing is certain – you will find the peace and
tranquillity of water an almost irresistible attraction

and you will find yourself thinking over
many garden problems at the waterside.

A LATIN PRIMER

Horizontalis Depressus

Dissectum Paniculata

Spectabilis Horridus

Buxifolius Filiformis

Williamsii Carnia

Argentea Vulgaris

Fruticans Pyramidalis

Pungens Prostratum

Robinia Floribunda

Radiata Neglectus

Fragrans Tortuosa

Flava Superba

Argutifolius Fistulosis

Alpestris Laxifolius

Monstrosa Impressus

Sistus Curiosa

Ovalifolium Longiflora

THE FIRESIDE
JUNGLE

Indoor plants can do much to improve the
visual appearance of your rooms . . .

but specimens should never be introduced
unless you know how to look after them.

Overwatering is a main cause of plant failure

and incorrect feeding can affect them adversely.

A smoky atmosphere is detrimental to pot plants . . .

whilst central heating is inclined to loosen their leaves.

Beware of introducing pests into the house
with new specimens . . .

and if they appear – destroy them at once.

See that your pets are well protected before using
chemical sprays.

Make sure each plant is suitable for the place
where it is kept.

A GARDENER'S
CALENDAR

JANUARY

This is the most convenient time to work out
your plans for the year.

Look for some out-of-the-way corner

and start your compost heap.

If your fish pool is covered with ice . . .

make a hole in it.

Keep an eye open for pests.

FEBRUARY

This is often a wet month so spike your lawns all over
to improve drainage.

Make a note of places where paths
have become slippery . . .

go out and repair them before they cause trouble.

Your snowdrops will be looking their best now.

Plant rose trees in a sunny part of the garden.

Make sure your geraniums have not damped off.

MARCH

Give support to anything disturbed by the wind.

Repair anything lifted by frost.

Look out for damage by hail.

Fill idle hours by making your own rustic seat.

Use it when you want to relax.

Burn all your garden rubbish.

APRIL

Your lawn will have started to grow now.

Get your mower out of the shed.

Try to put the other things back.

Start up the engine.

Try to repair it.

Send away mower for servicing.
Get your scythe out of the shed.

MAY

The birds will be a delight this month.

Provide them with plenty of nesting places.

On no account disturb the young.

Remove plants from rockery after flowering
and split them up.

Hand pollinate your fruit trees.

Dress with calamine lotion and get to bed.

JUNE

Aphis, millipedes, weevils, scab, blackleg, sawfly, thrips, pea moths, mealy bugs and other pests will be active.

Make a careful study of these creatures

and use every means to combat them.

There are many potent chemicals on the market

but private theories are often preferred.

Find out why your mower has not been returned.

JULY

Drought in the garden can be a serious problem
this month.

**Small amounts of liquid will merely
bring roots to the surface**

but it is an offence to use a hosepipe
without permission from the local authority.

Break up the hard soil around plants

and do everything possible to provide moisture . . .

then get under cover before you are struck by lightning.

AUGUST

An all-out effort will be needed to keep control now.
You should not have booked your holiday this month.

Try to find a friend who will keep an eye on things while you are away.

On no account let the neighbour's dog see you go.

Don't leave produce behind you to perish.

Once you are away – relax completely . . .

you'll need all your energy when you get home.

SEPTEMBER

All the familiar signs of harvest are with us once more.

Lift your main crop of potatoes.

Take care not to bruise ripe fruit.

Attend to wall climbers.

Clear out exhausted annuals.

Dispose of unproductive fruit trees.

OCTOBER

Brush all leaves into a neat pile to rot.
They will make valuable plant food.

Watch them blow all over the garden again.

Sweep them up and set fire to them.

Try to extinguish the potting shed.

Brush wood ash into a neat pile – it will make
valuable plant food.

Watch it blow all over the garden again.

NOVEMBER

Your lawn will have stopped growing now.

Your mower will be returned . . .

and your neighbour will borrow it.

Put down cloches to provide protection
from worsening weather.

Examine stored vegetables and throw out those
which show signs of rotting.

Beware of unexploded fireworks when
burning rubbish.

DECEMBER

Neglect of the garden now will mean hard work
next season – so keep at it.

Don't forget the birds – they are having a
hard time of it.

The festive season brings its own interesting
little chores . . .

. . . and well earned rewards.

The snow will be deep now –
get out into the garden . . .

Lie down – have a rest.